The Girl in the Yellow Dress

The Girl in the Yellow Dress

Poems by

Toni Ortner

Cover design by Shay Culligan
Cover image by Toni Ortner
Author photo by Coni Richards

ISBN: 978-1-63980-664-5

Kelsay Books
502 South 1040 East, A-119
American Fork, Utah 84003
Kelsaybooks.com

For My Daughter, Lisa

Acknowledgments

Versions of these poems previously appeared in these publications, some my own:

Black Sun, New Moon (Special Women's Edition of Hyperion, Carolina Wren Press, 1980): "I want to write this morning about a Japanese Stone Garden," "This morning I can clearly hear you laughing," "You of the unformed eye"

To an Imaginary Lover (The Morgan Press, 1975): "Your Numbers Are Not in the Wires," "All I Have," "This Poem is Open," "Desires"

Life, Generations, Dancing (privately printed, 1980): "No one would have known," "There is a woman knocking on my door," "I dreamed there was a blackened city," "As I recall you were always stubborn too," "When Daddy sat by your hospital bed," "When you are gone, mother"

Contents

New Year's Day (January, 1975)

Holding our daughter by her hands
we trudge through drifts of sparkling snow.

The sun directly overhead
melts the snow inch by inch.

Three hours left to build the promised snowman
with the ghosts of those we love.

The girl in the yellow dress designed by Betsy Johnson

The girl in the yellow dress swallowed fifty sleeping pills
all bones and dark eyes
wants to ride to the end of the line.

The pages of her books
gentle white translucent petals
fold softly around her cold wet skin.

In the evening she stands outside your lighted window
looking
in.

My Life Is Never Like a Japanese Stone Garden

I want to write this morning about a Japanese Stone Garden
clean smooth lines raked into sand
patterns of waves one could follow
to enter a formal pattern.

Somehow my life is never like this Japanese Stone Garden.
I am a woman.
I leak blood.
I sweat.
Right now
a tiny egg and sperm
attach to the wall of my uterus
settle in for nine months of moons
white cord stronger thicker   than your wrist.

All I Have

All I have is my breasts
and they are small and hard.
This is what I have to say to you.
I have held it a long time
with no one to say it to
and this is a way of beginning.

All I have is my eyes.
They are brown and ordinary.
Sometimes I will be able to see the trees
talk to you about the meaning of the trees
sometimes I will be able to examine the moss on the trees
take photographs of the trees and make poems about the trees
but sometimes even with the tree right in front of me
I won't be able to see them.

I can't promise not to cry.
Sometimes I will be terribly
angry
slam doors
smash chairs and China.

All I have is my arms
they are thin
but strong   can hold much
and let go.

All I have is my legs and the door
between
that can swing open.

All I have is my heart
red and beating wildly.

All I have is my freckles and skin
liver and milk and blood
and something wild you can hold

if you
will.

Your Numbers Are Not in the Wires

Early this evening the telephone rang.
When I picked it up, I heard nothing
but the sound of breathing.

Signing off.
Over and out.

All day I stumble around
dialing your number inside my head.
Seven simple digits flaming like fire. A simple flick of the wrist
and I could hear your voice on the other end of the wire
saying hello blankly across the city
without inference
or accusation
asking mildly
who it was.

Useless to call
when I cannot identify myself
either.

Someone has been phoning me for the past week
at the same time each day.
Two short rings followed by a long silence.
A radio signal from Sirius.
What good would it do to plead or shout
when I have said more than I should.

I realize if I had never known you
I would have been forced to imagine you
of
necessity
like a woman with nine fingers.

Pity, your numbers are not in the wires.

This Poem Is Open

This poem is open
the lines reach out
willow trees rush in
there is a shining river
the waters are silver
it flows past your door
in summer in autumn in spring in winter
you sit by the window
your eyes
closed.

Desires

Desires, small enough to be missed
pile up slowly between us
form a wall
we will never get through.
I stare at your shoes as you talk.
You believe they remind me of a phallic object.
I do not correct you.
I am remembering how when I was four
and my father was away on a trip
I used to walk gingerly into his closet
stare at his shoes
brown and navy oxfords polished
smelling sweetly of leather
me kneeling before them
holding them tenderly against my cheek
like delicate rare
flowers
I dared not crush.

I can clearly hear you

This morning I can clearly hear you laughing
        you, of the unformed mouth
                you, still without an eye.

I debate whether or not to make you exist
while underneath these words
minute by minute
cells automatically divide.

Continents shift
while in glass towers
we construct our maps.

Tunnel of Love

You of the unformed eye
I can more easily imagine a cup or broken saucer.

I am a baby factory.
I am a baby machine.
I contain eggs smaller than the heads of pins.

Inside the hallway of mirrors you cling
lit red by the unnatural garish light of blood.

This is the tunnel of love.
We cling to one another
half shaking with fright and delight
glide over dark waters
waiting to break through into day
where we can see one another's freckles.

Mr. Death

You stand behind me smiling quietly.
You don't like the way I kiss.
You don't like the taste of my lips.

Mr. Death, come closer.
What color are your eyes?
Are they the blue ones that flashed like semaphores
as the train rushed through railroad stations?

Mr. Death, your language it too guttural.
You eat small children.

Mr. Death,
You are infatuated with yourself.
You think you've bagged them all
Li Po
Beethoven
Brahms.

You got a lot of publicity
from the earthquake in Guatemala
mothers huddled with babies
against shaking walls of buildings.

I've had lovers
but they were hot, not cold like you.
They didn't smell of rot.

You loan me out
collect interest.

You bastard, dressed in black.
Did you think I would forget you?

Horse Dream

By late fall
horses have
made
meadow
bare stubble
punctuated by
stones.

content
lick
white frost
surrounded
by clouds of
steam.

Bell Hollow Road

Trees
fallen seeds
sprung from the most improbably places
cling
tenacious.

Three solid gray trunks
march up the hill
in an unbroken line
to the house
whose inhabitants sleep
through the long night
of their lives.

Singles/Doubles

Objects without masters confront us with a life of their own.

Grief fits me like a glove.

In my dreams
twilight and old guns.

Sorrow comes and goes
like an old dog,

Snow
sifts space
against the evening star.

Jazz Monologue by Max Cole

Yes honey, the news just came through from the Reverend Ginsel pastor to the jazz community that Jimmy Garrison died although the news is not yet confirmed by any sources. Did you know the rate of addiction in New York is increasing on account of unemployment? The ones who are here try to keep a stiff upper lip, keep on truckin. Even the housewives in the suburbs who can't buy filet mignon anymore recall the wire photos of black babies with swollen bellies in Biafra. Where do we all go? For sure it's not over the rainbow the way Judy Garland told us. Some of us get out of bed singing at the top of our lungs just to rise on up. The poets try to write poems. The musicians try to make a little music, but their horns sound like high-pitched screams and moans. Nothin' for dinner but eggs if you're lucky. It's not only old people who fill up their carts with dog food at the A& P. In India they live in houses made of dry dung. The scientists at Yale are experimenting with electronic brain simulation that can make a starving rat avoid a plate of food to have his pleasure center stimulated. They will begin a few experiments like these on human beings incarcerated by the state. A famous prophet named Edgar Cayce dreamed he was flying over New York City, and it was underwater with the blue Atlantic washing cleanly in. We have lost the use of our brains although we have developed a huge stockpile of nuclear weapons. Remember the demise of the dinosaurs. The sky is blue. The grass is green. Now we will play a little tune for the late Jimmy Garrison who was famous for playing with the late great Charlie Parker. Stop crying, dear.

All I Wanted

All I wanted
was the house on the hill I drew
two windows
smoke curling from the chimney like a smile
tulips blooming by the front door
someone tended.

Dream of Football

I am on a football field along with the others, but they are men. I would think this is a funny story someone told me, but I can't wake up. I am running as fast as I can. I can't remember the signals and never know the plays but pretend to go along with them. Heavy bodies charge past. I am tempted to laugh. All I know is four feet of mud. The bleachers could be full or empty. All I can see is legs running on either side. Where the goal is I don't know. It must be in the direction we are running.

Suddenly, I hold the ball. The others shout. Now that I've got the ball, I keep on running.

When you are gone

When you are gone, mother
I will picture you walking on the road to Damascus
under a clear blue sky and brilliant white sun
blueberries to stain your tongue
shadows cast by cypress trees   holy candles flickering.

Since your story is mine
I will learn to speak again to tell it.

I tell you this now mother so you will not worry.

Before Surgery

No one would have known
how nervous you were except me.

You drove on the wrong side of the road
for five minutes before you noticed,

You stood in pouring rain
to dig out blue violets
from your garden
to transplant into mine.

You kept asking me the time.

Recall

As I recall
you were always stubborn.

One night when Daddy was watching television
did not respond to your question
you walked in front of the set
with the spikes of your high-heeled shoes
kicked the screen in.

By Your Hospital Bed

When Daddy sat by your hospital bed
he was silent a long time
watching fluid dripping from the plastic bag
into the vein in your arm
watching your white face
swim under drugs.

        White petal floating in wild water
        white petal drifting downstream
        spinning   swirled round   sucked under.

Suddenly, he muttered to himself
how you couldn't kick the bucket yet.

He wanted to needle you into admitting all
your lovers.

Blackened City

I dreamed there was a blackened city
hot pavements smoking
vacant lots in which weeds sang.

Through this city I walked
in bare feet
soles burnt

searching for a lost child
I found
buried like a broken toy under rubble.

O ruined cities of my dreams
in which I wander forever
to salvage
    the child who will not flower from my seed
    the child whose body is discovered in the airplane wreckage
    the promise burnt to ash.

If I Stood Still

If I stood still, I might hear a quiet sigh.
It is not the swollen stream flooding its banks.
It is not the rainwater streaming down the eaves.

It is the sigh of the lost child.

I Have Tried to Speak

Lisa,

My words mean nothing until you translate.
There are no correct answers like the teacher told you.

My language is my own.
I apologize for its limitations.

I have tried to speak
forced out syllables like hard stones.

In the cold space between the stars
it is impossible to whistle any tune.

There Is a Woman

There is a woman knocking on my door
  I hear her crying, but her cries are very soft
  she hasn't much strength left
  I cannot hear her words
  her tongue has been cut off.

I keep on talking
safe inside the room.

There is a woman knocking on my door
trying to get in.

She does not have my education.
She does not have my money.
She does not have a husband.
Her body is bruised and beaten.

There is a woman knocking on my door
day after day
night after night
while I keep on talking
safe inside the room

until I wonder
which one of us is safe
which one knocking at the door
which one locked inside the room.

Snapped the Lock

I've snapped the lock.
Now I can carry you wherever I go
folded neatly, little fish
wrapped in layers of flesh.

Sleep my child sleep
curled up with your thumb for nine months.

This is the safest place you will be until your death.

Let the men have their guns.
I will eat mountains to feed you.

About the Author

Toni Ortner, who lives in Vermont, has had 30 books published by small presses. *The Van Gogh Notebook* will be published next by the Dancing Girl Press. She taught in the English Department of the University of Connecticut as well as other colleges. Her magazine *Connections* was one of the first to publish work mainly by women; copies of it are at Poet's House in New York.

She was Vice President of Write Action Inc., a nonprofit group that supports writers in southern Vermont and the area of Brattleboro and ran the Write Action Radio Hour on the local radio station for many years where she interviewed writers and they read their work. During the height of Covid she hosted the Putney Writers Salon on Zoom.

You can find her books and reviews on her website:
toniortner.com

www.ingramcontent.com/pod-product-compliance
Lightning Source LLC
Chambersburg PA
CBHW071116090426
42737CB00013B/2596

9 781639 806645